The Ultimate Keyboard SCALE CHART

Introduction

The *Ultimate Keyboard Scale Chart* has been created to assist you in learning to play today's most commonly used scales. It is a fast and fun way to gain instant access to 120 essential scale patterns: just look up a scale and you can easily find out how to play it.

This book will not only show you the different scales and their locations, but will also provide the basic rules behind *how* and *why* each scale is constructed. This approach to learning will greatly enhance your playing and understanding of scales.

How to Use This Book

To use the chart on the following pages, simply find the root of the scale along the top of the chart, and the scale type (major, minor, etc.) in the column at the left. Read across and down to find the correct scale. (Note: for melodic minor, only the ascending pattern is shown—descend using the natural minor pattern. All other scales are the same in either direction.)

Each scale is playable by either the right or left hand, or both at once. A helpful fingering guide is also included.

C major

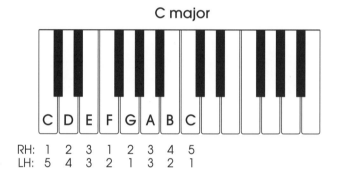

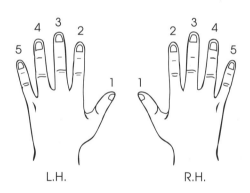

L.H.   R.H.

ISBN 0-634-01442-0

HAL•LEONARD® CORPORATION
7777 W. BLUEMOUND RD. P.O. BOX 13819 MILWAUKEE, WI 53213

Visit Hal Leonard Online at
www.halleonard.com

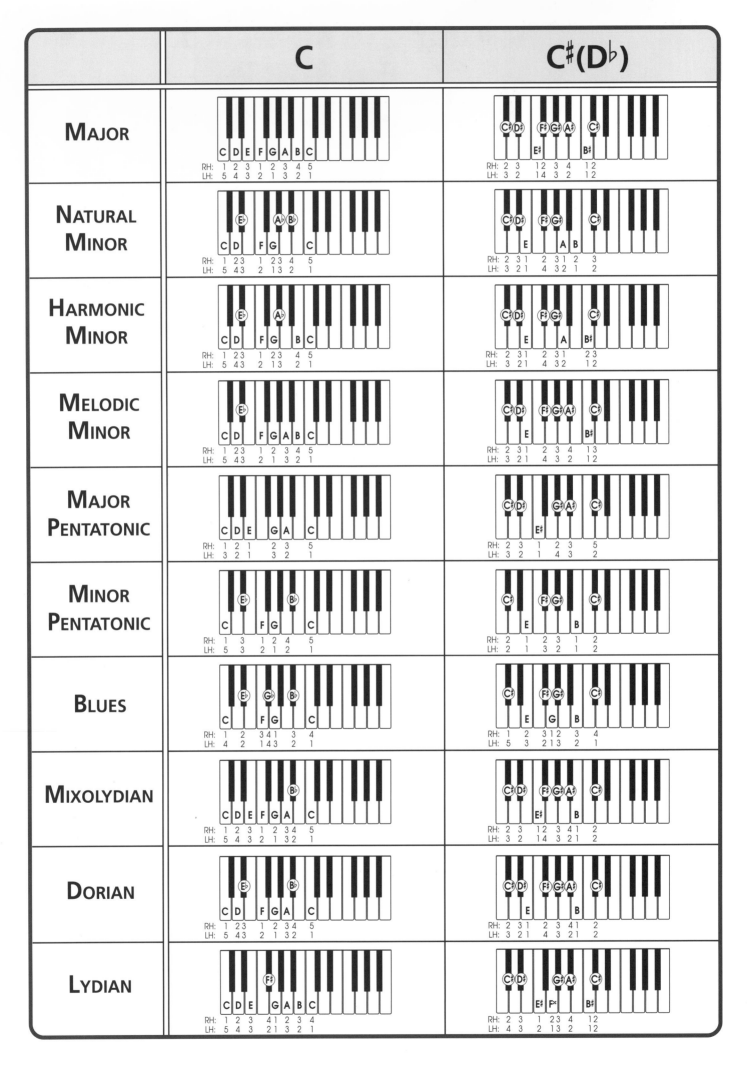

Scale	D	E♭
MAJOR	D E F♯ G A B C♯ D RH: 1 2 3 1 2 3 4 5 LH: 5 4 3 2 1 3 2 1	E♭ F G A♭ B♭ C D E♭ RH: 3 1 2 3 4 1 2 3 LH: 3 2 1 4 3 2 1 2
NATURAL MINOR	D E F G A B♭ C D RH: 1 2 3 1 2 3 4 5 LH: 5 4 3 2 1 3 2 1	E♭ F G♭ A♭ B♭ C♭ D♭ E♭ RH: 3 1 2 3 4 1 2 3 LH: 2 1 4 3 2 1 3 2
HARMONIC MINOR	D E F G A B♭ C♯ D RH: 1 2 3 1 2 3 4 5 LH: 5 4 3 2 1 3 2 1	E♭ F G♭ A♭ B♭ C♭ D E♭ RH: 3 1 2 3 4 1 2 3 LH: 2 1 4 3 2 1 3 2
MELODIC MINOR	D E F G A B C♯ D RH: 1 2 3 1 2 3 4 5 LH: 5 4 3 2 1 3 2 1	E♭ F G♭ A♭ B♭ C D E♭ RH: 3 1 2 3 4 1 2 3 LH: 2 1 4 3 2 1 3 2
MAJOR PENTATONIC	D E F♯ A B D RH: 1 2 3 1 2 4 LH: 4 3 2 1 2 1	E♭ F G B♭ C E♭ RH: 2 1 2 3 1 2 LH: 3 2 1 2 1 2
MINOR PENTATONIC	D F G A C D RH: 1 2 3 1 2 3 LH: 4 2 1 3 2 1	E♭ G♭ A♭ B♭ D♭ E♭ RH: 1 2 3 1 2 3 LH: 3 2 1 3 2 1
BLUES	D F G A♭ A C D RH: 1 2 3 4 1 3 4 LH: 4 2 1 4 3 2 1	E♭ G♭ A♭ B♭♭ B♭ D♭ E♭ RH: 1 2 3 1 2 3 4 LH: 5 3 2 1 3 2 1
MIXOLYDIAN	D E F♯ G A B C D RH: 1 2 3 1 2 3 4 5 LH: 5 4 3 2 1 3 2 1	E♭ F G A♭ B♭ C D♭ E♭ RH: 3 1 2 3 4 1 2 3 LH: 3 2 1 3 2 1
DORIAN	D E F G A B C D RH: 1 2 3 1 2 3 4 5 LH: 5 4 3 2 1 3 2 1	E♭ F G♭ A♭ B♭ C D♭ E♭ RH: 3 1 2 3 4 1 2 3 LH: 2 1 4 3 2 1 3 2
LYDIAN	D E F♯ G♯ A B C♯ D RH: 1 2 3 4 1 2 3 4 LH: 5 4 3 2 1 3 2 1	E♭ F G A B♭ C D E♭ RH: 3 1 2 3 4 1 2 3 LH: 4 3 2 1 3 2 1 2

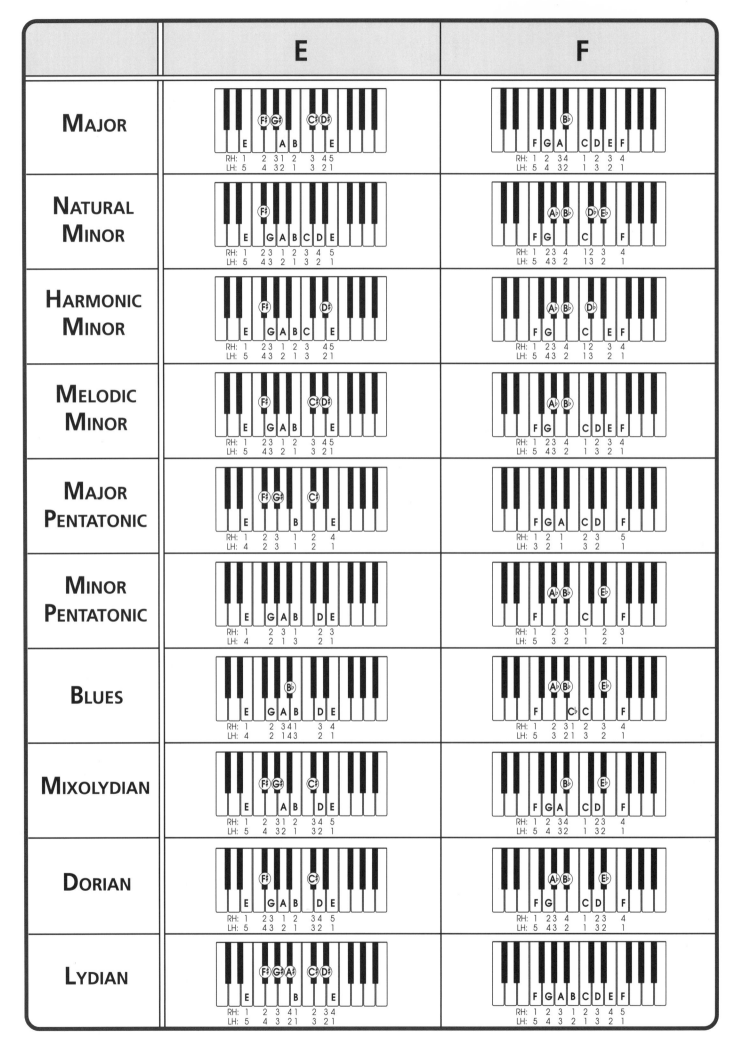

	F♯ (G♭)	G
MAJOR	F♯ G♯ A♯ B C♯ D♯ E♯ F♯ — RH: 2 3 41 2 3 1 2 / LH: 4 3 21 3 2 1 2	G A B C D E F♯ G — RH: 1 2 3 1 2 3 45 / LH: 5 4 3 2 1 3 21
NATURAL MINOR	F♯ G♯ A B C♯ D E F♯ — RH: 2 31 2 31 2 3 / LH: 4 32 1 32 1 2	G A B♭ C D E♭ F G — RH: 1 23 1 23 4 5 / LH: 5 43 2 13 2 1
HARMONIC MINOR	F♯ G♯ A B C♯ D E♯ F♯ — RH: 2 31 2 31 23 / LH: 4 32 1 32 12	G A B♭ C D E♭ F♯ G — RH: 1 23 1 23 45 / LH: 5 43 2 13 21
MELODIC MINOR	F♯ G♯ A B C♯ D♯ E♯ F♯ — RH: 2 31 2 3 4 / LH: 4 32 1 3 2 12	G A B♭ C D E F♯ G — RH: 1 23 1 2 3 45 / LH: 5 43 2 1 3 21
MAJOR PENTATONIC	F♯ G♯ A♯ C♯ D♯ F♯ — RH: 2 3 4 1 2 3 / LH: 4 3 2 1 2 1	G A B D E G — RH: 1 2 1 2 3 5 / LH: 3 2 1 3 2 1
MINOR PENTATONIC	F♯ A B C♯ E F♯ — RH: 2 1 2 3 1 2 / LH: 4 2 1 2 1 2	G B♭ C D F G — RH: 1 3 1 2 4 5 / LH: 4 2 1 4 2 1
BLUES	F♯ A B C C♯ E F♯ — RH: 1 2 3 12 3 4 / LH: 5 3 2 13 2 1	G B♭ C D♭ D F G — RH: 1 2 34 1 3 4 / LH: 4 2 143 2 1
MIXOLYDIAN	F♯ G♯ A♯ B C♯ D♯ E F♯ — RH: 2 3 41 2 31 2 / LH: 4 3 21 3 21 2	G A B C D E F G — RH: 1 2 3 1 2 3 45 / LH: 5 4 3 2 1 3 21
DORIAN	F♯ G♯ A B C♯ D♯ E F♯ — RH: 2 31 2 3 41 2 / LH: 4 32 1 3 21 2	G A B♭ C D E F G — RH: 1 23 1 2 3 45 / LH: 5 43 2 1 3 21
LYDIAN	F♯ G♯ A♯ B♯ C♯ D♯ E♯ F♯ — RH: 2 3 4 1 2 3 12 / LH: 4 3 2 13 2 12	G A B C♯ D E F♯ G — RH: 1 2 3 41 2 34 5 / LH: 5 4 3 21 3 21

5

	A♭ (G♯)	A
MAJOR	A♭ B♭ C D♭ E♭ F G A♭ RH: 3 4 1 2 3 1 2 3 LH: 3 2 1 4 3 2 1 3	A B C♯ D E F♯ G♯ A RH: 1 2 3 1 2 3 4 5 LH: 5 4 3 2 1 3 2 1
NATURAL MINOR	A♭ B♭ C♭ D♭ E♭ F♭ G♭ A♭ RH: 3 4 1 2 3 1 2 3 LH: 3 2 1 3 2 1 3 2	A B C D E F G A RH: 1 2 3 1 2 3 4 5 LH: 5 4 3 2 1 3 2 1
HARMONIC MINOR	A♭ B♭ C♭ D♭ E♭ F♭ G A♭ RH: 3 4 1 2 3 1 2 3 LH: 3 2 1 3 2 1 3 2	A B C D E F G♯ A RH: 1 2 3 1 2 3 4 5 LH: 5 4 3 2 1 3 2 1
MELODIC MINOR	A♭ B♭ C♭ D♭ E♭ F G A♭ RH: 3 4 1 2 3 1 2 3 LH: 3 2 1 3 2 1 3 2	A B C D E F♯ G♯ A RH: 1 2 3 1 2 3 4 5 LH: 5 4 3 2 1 3 2 1
MAJOR PENTATONIC	A♭ B♭ C E♭ F A♭ RH: 2 3 1 2 3 5 LH: 3 2 1 2 1	A B C♯ E F♯ A RH: 1 2 3 1 2 4 LH: 4 2 3 1 2 1
MINOR PENTATONIC	A♭ C♭ D♭ E♭ G♭ A♭ RH: 2 1 2 3 4 5 LH: 2 1 4 3 2 1	A C D E G A RH: 1 2 3 1 2 3 LH: 4 2 1 3 2 1
BLUES	A♭ C♭ D♭ E♭♭ E♭ G♭ A♭ RH: 1 2 3 1 2 3 4 LH: 5 3 2 1 4 3 2	A C D E♭ E G A RH: 1 2 3 4 1 3 4 LH: 4 2 1 4 3 2 1
MIXOLYDIAN	A♭ B♭ C D♭ E♭ F G♭ A♭ RH: 3 4 1 2 3 1 2 3 LH: 3 2 1 3 2 1 3 2	A B C♯ D E F♯ G A RH: 1 2 3 1 2 3 4 5 LH: 5 4 3 2 1 3 2 1
DORIAN	A♭ B♭ C♭ D♭ E♭ F G♭ A♭ RH: 3 4 1 2 3 1 2 3 LH: 3 2 1 3 2 1 3 2	A B C D E F♯ G A RH: 1 2 3 1 2 3 4 5 LH: 5 4 3 2 1 3 2 1
LYDIAN	A♭ B♭ C D E♭ F G A♭ RH: 3 4 1 2 3 1 2 3 LH: 4 3 2 1 3 2 1 2	A B C♯ D♯ E F♯ G♯ A RH: 1 2 3 4 1 2 3 4 LH: 5 4 3 2 1 3 2 1

	B♭	B
MAJOR	Notes: B♭ C D E♭ F G A B♭ RH: 2 1 2 3 1 2 3 4 LH: 3 2 1 4 3 2 1 2	Notes: B C♯ D♯ E F♯ G♯ A♯ B RH: 1 2 3 1 2 3 4 5 LH: 4 3 2 1 4 3 2 1
NATURAL MINOR	Notes: B♭ C D♭ E♭ F G♭ A♭ B♭ RH: 2 1 2 3 1 2 3 4 LH: 2 1 3 2 1 4 3 2	Notes: B C♯ D E F♯ G A B RH: 1 2 3 1 2 3 4 5 LH: 4 3 2 1 4 3 2 1
HARMONIC MINOR	Notes: B♭ C D♭ E♭ F G♭ A B♭ RH: 2 1 2 3 1 2 3 4 LH: 2 1 3 2 1 4 3 2	Notes: B C♯ D E F♯ G A♯ B RH: 1 2 3 1 2 3 4 5 LH: 4 3 2 1 4 3 2 1
MELODIC MINOR	Notes: B♭ C D♭ E♭ F G A B♭ RH: 2 1 2 3 1 2 3 4 LH: 2 1 3 2 1 4 3 2	Notes: B C♯ D E F♯ G♯ A♯ B RH: 1 2 3 1 2 3 4 5 LH: 4 3 2 1 4 3 2 1
MAJOR PENTATONIC	Notes: B♭ C D F G B♭ RH: 2 1 2 3 1 2 LH: 3 2 1 3 2 1	Notes: B C♯ D♯ F♯ G♯ B RH: 1 2 3 1 2 4 LH: 4 3 2 1 2 1
MINOR PENTATONIC	Notes: B♭ D♭ E♭ F A♭ B♭ RH: 2 3 4 1 2 3 LH: 4 3 2 1 3 2	Notes: B D E F♯ A B RH: 1 2 3 4 1 2 LH: 4 2 1 3 2 1
BLUES	Notes: B♭ D♭ E♭ F♭ F A♭ B♭ RH: 2 3 4 1 2 3 4 LH: 4 3 2 1 4 3 2	Notes: B D E F F♯ A B RH: 1 2 3 1 2 3 4 LH: 5 3 2 1 3 2 1
MIXOLYDIAN	Notes: B♭ C D E♭ F G A♭ B♭ RH: 2 1 2 3 1 2 3 4 LH: 3 2 1 3 2 1 3 2	Notes: B C♯ D♯ E F♯ G♯ A B RH: 1 2 3 1 2 3 4 5 LH: 4 3 2 1 4 3 2 1
DORIAN	Notes: B♭ C D♭ E♭ F G A♭ B♭ RH: 2 1 2 3 1 2 3 4 LH: 2 1 4 3 2 1 3 2	Notes: B C♯ D E F♯ G♯ A B RH: 1 2 3 1 2 3 4 5 LH: 4 3 2 1 4 3 2 1
LYDIAN	Notes: B♭ C D E F G A B♭ RH: 2 1 2 3 1 2 3 4 LH: 4 3 2 1 3 2 1 2	Notes: B C♯ D♯ E♯ F♯ G♯ A♯ B RH: 1 2 3 1 2 3 4 5 LH: 4 3 2 1 4 3 2 1

ABOUT SCALES

What Is a Scale?

A **scale** is a series of notes arranged in ascending or descending order. (The word "scale" comes from the Latin *scala*, which means "ladder.") Scales are important to know on the keyboard, especially when creating riffs, licks and solos.

How Are Scales Formed?

Scales are constructed using a combination of *whole steps* and *half steps*. (On the keyboard, a *half step* is the distance between two immediately adjacent keys, whether white or black; a *whole step* is two half steps.) Perhaps the most common scale is the *major scale*, shown here in C:

C MAJOR SCALE

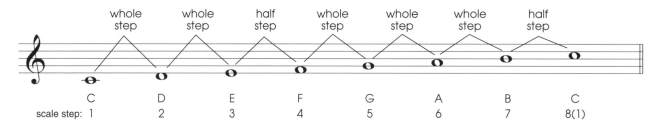

Notice the pattern above: *whole–whole–half–whole–whole–whole–half*. This is the "major scale" step pattern, which can be applied to any root note to create any major scale—C major, D major, E major, etc.

Notice also that each scale step above is numbered: 1–2–3–4–5–6–7–1. The chart to the right is a construction summary of the scale types in this book (based on the key of C only). Use the numeric formulas to determine the notes of a particular scale. For example, based on a C root, 1–2–♭3–4–5–♭6–♭7–1 would mean to play C–D–E♭–F–G–A♭–B♭–C—in other words, a natural minor scale.

SCALE TYPE	FORMULA	NOTE NAMES
major	1-2-3-4-5-6-7-1	C-D-E-F-G-A-B-C
natural minor	1-2-♭3-4-5-♭6-♭7-1	C-D-E♭-F-G-A♭-B♭-C
harmonic minor	1-2-♭3-4-5-♭6-7-1	C-D-E♭-F-G-A♭-B-C
melodic minor	1-2-♭3-4-5-6-7-1	C-D-E♭-F-G-A-B-C
major pentatonic	1-2-3-5-6-1	C-D-E-G-A-C
minor pentatonic	1-♭3-4-5-♭7-1	C-E♭-F-G-B♭-C
blues	1-♭3-4-♭5-5-♭7-1	C-D-E♭-F-G♭-A-B♭-C
Mixolydian	1-2-3-4-5-6-♭7-1	C-D-E-F-G-A-B♭-C
Dorian	1-2-♭3-4-5-6-♭7-1	C-D-E♭-F-G-A-B♭-C
Lydian	1-2-3-♯4-5-6-7-1	C-D-E-F♯-G-A-B-C

How Are Scales Used?

Here are a few points to keep in mind when improvising with scales:

- You don't have to play scales from root to root; this is simply the way that they are best demonstrated. The notes of a scale can be played *in any order*, and you don't need to use them all. The root is often the most important note.

- Try to choose a scale that goes with the overall key of a song, or song section, not just with a single chord; this will allow you to improvise most effectively, using a single scale pattern.

- In general, when playing in a *major key*, try any of the following scales: **major, major pentatonic, blues, Mixolydian,** or **Lydian.**

- When playing in a *minor key*, try these: **minor, minor pentatonic, harmonic minor, melodic minor, blues,** or **Dorian.**